How to Be a Better You
(without booze)

Joshua Wade Miller

How to Be a Better You (without booze)
Copyright © [2018] by [Joshua Wade Miller]

For information, contact Josh at [josh@howtobeabetteryou.today].

This book was inspired by my experience at the Institute for Integrative Nutrition® (IIN), where I received my training in holistic wellness and health coaching. IIN offers a truly comprehensive Health Coach Training Program that invites students to deeply explore the things that are most nourishing to them.

From the physical aspects of nutrition and eating wholesome foods that work best for each individual person, to the concept of Primary Food – the idea that everything in life, including our spirituality, career, relationships, and fitness contributes to our inner and outer health – IIN helped me reach optimal health and balance. This inner journey unleashed the passion that compels me to share what I've learned and inspire others. Beyond personal health, IIN offers training in health coaching, as well as business and marketing. Students who choose to pursue this field professionally complete the program equipped with the communication skills and branding knowledge they need to create a fulfilling career encouraging and supporting others in reaching their own health goals. From renowned wellness experts as Visiting Teachers to the convenience of their online learning platform, this school has changed my life, and I believe it will do the same for you. I invite you to learn more about the Institute for Integrative Nutrition and explore how the Health Coach Training Program can help you transform your life. Feel free to call (844) 315-8546 to learn more.

Table of Contents

Introduction

Welcome to How To Be a Better You (Without Booze)! I'm so glad that you found this book and I truly hope that it helps you to become a better version of you. This book is in no way meant to be coming from a 'holier than thou' place. I am simply sharing some basic common sense that has worked for me. This is your life, and I don't know you or where you are coming from. This book is meant to be a simple step-by-step guide to help you find healthier alternatives to alcohol.

You may not have issues with alcohol like I did. Most people can drink in moderation without it taking over their lives and becoming a huge problem. You may be one of the millions that do have issues with booze and may be searching for a way out, but aren't really sure where to start. If that is you, then this is the book for you. Many people seek refuge from booze through Alcoholics Anonymous (AA) or church or other programs that I did not personally go through. Therefore, I'm not all about complete sobriety according to those ideas.

If you are the kind of person who can drink responsibly, then this may not be the book for you. In fact, it may not resonate with you at all. And that is totally okay. I'm not claiming to be any kind of authority on this subject, because I can only speak for myself. And since I am the authority on myself, all I can tell you is this technique I'm going to share with you has worked for me.

I did this with my own willpower and some minor adjustments to my lifestyle. Okay maybe they were major adjustments, but they started as minor and slowly became major. And the good news is, that it was much easier than I realized it was going to be too.

If you are anything like I was, then you just don't know when to stop once you start drinking. After many years of alcohol abuse, I found myself spiraling out of control. I was in a self-destructive pattern that ultimately led to me hurting others around me. It was a process that accumulated over the years, and I didn't even realize it was happening until it was too late. The damage had already been done, and I was forced to look at the problems that I created for my loved ones and myself.

If you are reading this, then it's likely that you have been struggling with overconsumption and may be seeking guidance. I don't claim to be an expert, but I did figure out another system that has worked for me for over eight years so far.

My approach comes from a place of healthy choices that led to more healthy choices. It is simply about a brain shift that helps keep you going down a healthy path instead of a destructive path. This approach has worked for me, and the desire to drink has completely subsided. I didn't need to go to meetings and work a program to do this. That does work for many people, and I have the utmost respect for anyone who can use AA to stay sober. However, I personally feel that it can be counterproductive for many others.

We now live in the information age where we can find other alternatives. Our brains are malleable, and a simple shift in thought patterns can make all the difference we need. I incorporate steps to success that are not meant to drastically change your life. It's about making healthier choices that will keep you focused on staying away from alcohol.

It's more about going inward as opposed to the need to share your story with strangers all the time. It's about shifting your brain patterns, so you think about healing yourself with water, exercise, whole foods, meditation, and love. Perhaps even a little cannabis now and then. It's not about reliving your old story day after day so that you remain in this place of feeling like you are somehow broken. I don't believe in the idea that you can't do it alone, because you can. In fact I recommend doing it alone. That's not to say that you should be lonely through this process though. You will also need support from others too, but ultimately this is a journey to take on your own.

I wrote this book as a short, practical guide to your evolution to a better version of yourself. It shouldn't be overwhelming as these steps are short and easy to digest. If you apply these steps, it will help to lead you to a longer, happier, healthier life. And trust me when I say that removing booze (if it is controlling your life) is the best way to start this process. Enjoy!

Wake-up Call

Did you get drunk again last night? Did your friends call to tell you how drunk you were? Did they tell you stories that you don't remember? Like how you got home? Are you trying to remember if you drove or not? Do you know where your car might be parked right now? Maybe you're still drunk from last night. Or maybe you just started drinking before you picked up this book to read. Whatever the case may be, I'm glad you decided to pick it up. Or pull it up on your computer screen. Because I was there too and I get it. I drank heavily for over half my life. I over indulged on a daily basis for many years. But then I woke up. I woke up to a new healthy, stress free life. And I'm going to tell you how I did it.

At this point in my life, I can't even imagine having another drink. The thought of it just doesn't appeal to me anymore. Maybe one of these days I could have a glass of wine with dinner, but that would be more for health reasons than for the reason I used to drink, which was to get drunk. That was the sole purpose for me.

I'm not sure about you, and how or why you drink, but

it's just not worth the so-called fun that you think you're having. Don't get me wrong, I know how fun drinking can be, but the long-term damage that is done to your body and mind only gets worse over time.

If you have ever seen the results of dementia, then that should be a good wake up call. It's devastating to watch someone losing memory. So many people are affected by dementia, and it's getting worse. Alzeheimer's is supposed to triple within the next twenty-five years. Triple! That's primarily because of sugar. In case you didn't know it, alcohol is sugar. But we don't think about the long-term effects when we are drinking ourselves stupid. It's too much fun. Until that one day when it becomes not so fun anymore.

Today we should all know better, but somehow, we just don't seem to. As long as you continue to drink like a fish, your later years are going to be miserable. You can pretty much count on that. However, if we just start implementing new habits earlier in life, then we can have quality years later in life.

I think a big reason most people drink these days is a combination of dealing with some kind of childhood issues, and the fact that alcohol is basically shoved down our throats from every direction. From our peers, to TV and movies, to billboards and magazines, or even the songs on the radio.

We have grown so accustomed to this notion that we can't socialize without alcohol. You want to go on a date or make out with someone? Let's get drunk first. You want to go to a birthday party or hang out with friends? Let's get wasted! You want to go out to dinner for business? Pour the wine!

Alcohol has been a part of our lives in some way or another from the moment we are born. And you may or may not have had parents that drink. Or drank, or drunk. I wasn't actually around alcohol too much as a child. My father was a drinker, but my mother left him when I was two years old. And she wasn't really much of a drinker other than an occasional glass of wine. It must have just been in my blood from my father's side.

I'm not really sure why I chose to drink. I was pretty popular in high school. I was even the vice president of my student body. So it wasn't out of insecurities for me. I think it was more about curiosity and the desire to fit in. I look back on those days, and I laugh, because peer pressure seems so silly to me now. But at that time, it is a huge part of our lives. The desire to fit in at those crucial teenage years is overwhelming. Since the law tells us that we can't do it legally until we turn twenty-one, the rebellious nature of teens is peaked. Curiosity kills the cat, and the liver, and ultimately the mind too.

Do you know why you drink? Because when you stop to think about it, you will realize that it's not entirely your fault. I mean obviously, it's you who ultimately made the decision to take that first drink. However, you have been programmed to think that drinking is cool or acceptable. And I'm going to let you in on a little secret. It's not really cool to get blackout drunk and cheat on your girlfriend with her best friend. Especially not right down the hall from that girlfriend who was asleep. Especially not when you're in your thirties. Yeah, I was that guy.

Countless lives have been lost due to alcohol. In fact, it's the leading cause of death for ages fifteen to twenty. How messed up is that? A drunk driver kills someone every forty-five minutes. I mean come on, that's crazy! Where are we going wrong as a society? It's not like we aren't told the dangers of drinking and driving. And yet it still happens all the time. Even with all these different ride sharing apps out there. It's crazy to think about how it starts at such a young age, and it continues to ruin so many lives for so long. It's just not right, and it's time for a change in this behavior.

Quick story. My ex-girlfriend and I were hit and almost killed by a drunk driver a few years ago. It was like a scene straight out of the "Fast and the Furious". We were coming home from work on Sunset Boulevard entering Beverly Hills and all of a sudden, a car came skidding out of control towards us. As we came to the turn (which is called "dead man's curve"), the car was air born and upside down falling onto us. His car rolled onto the front of my car and continued to flip two or three more times as he landed in someone's front yard. Fortunately, no one died, but my girlfriend had major surgery and will have a metal rod in her leg for the rest of her life. I suffered a fractured sternum and a broken foot, which was no picnic either.

This kid that hit us was twenty-one years old, and he was completely wasted. It was pretty amazing that any of us lived through it. In fact, the cops told us that it was the worst car accident they had ever seen. And this is in LA so you know they must have seen a LOT of accidents. I never found out what the guy's blood alcohol level was, but apparently, it was insanely high. He also had open containers in his car.

But here's the honest truth. I also had an open container in my car. I just wasn't drunk yet. I was on my way to get drunk though. This was my routine. I usually had a roadie with me. And I drove drunk more times than I can count. You might think this crash would've been a wake-up call. This wasn't what made me stop drinking though. In my mind, it was his fault because I wasn't drunk. And I was a safe driver, drunk or sober.

It's hard to believe how alcohol is still so accepted by society. I did it for nearly half my life, and if I didn't wake up, I would probably be dead.

Now I'm not trying to depress you on page 12 here. I honestly want this to be fun for you. I'm sure it seems impossible to have a good time without alcohol right now. Trust me; I know how fun alcohol can be. I have had some amazing times while I was wasted. However, it's been a much bigger blast to be alcohol free. And it can be for you too. It may seem weird to think of your life without it now, but once you make that decision to better yourself, you won't miss it either.

I'm going to assume that if you are reading this book that you may have come to the conclusion that you need to take a look at your alcohol issues. Maybe your life is completely out of control, or maybe you just can't figure out how to get yourself out of these patterns. Or maybe you are my Mom or friend reading this because you love me. Whatever the reason you are reading this, I want to congratulate you. For taking the time to recognize that you need some help or guidance. It's not easy to make this choice, so you deserve to be congratulated for that alone. The decision to see this through is entirely up to you. But I believe in you, and I know you can do it. If I can do it, then I know you can too.

This goes without saying, but everything you do in this life is up to you, and you alone have the power to change the course you are on. It just takes some tweaks to your current patterns. Tweaks that we will get into in depth later. Most of these tweaks are common sense too and won't require reinventing the wheel. Although common sense isn't really something that we have a lot of when we are drinking. Am I right?

At least I know I didn't have any common sense when I was drinking. I never fully understood why I couldn't stop my behavior. I would get completely shitfaced one night, and then instead of feeling regret, I would just do it all over again the next night. For years I would get drunk every single night. Sometimes I would have a somewhat clear recollection of the previous night's events, and other times I would blackout. Most days when I would go to my car, I would be like "Dude, Where's My Car"?

That's when I was living in Los Angeles and didn't have a parking space, so I would have to walk around my neighborhood multiple times to try and find my car. Not some of my proudest moments.

If you have ever lived in LA, then you may be familiar with the party scene there. And if you haven't lived there, then I'm sure you've heard about it. When you are trying to make it in the Hollywood business, there tends to be this idea that you need to go out and network. And in order to network, you feel like you need to fit into that scene. And alcohol is the courage juice that helps you feel connected, because everyone is doing it.

Looking back now, I realize that none of the people that I really needed to meet were anywhere near those parties and bars where I was trying to network. The real successful people were tucked away in their huge houses actually working. I also now realize that I needed to drink more to deal with some of the LA douchebaggery. Or douchebaggedness. Well, just plain douchery. And I got sucked right into it all. I thought I was out there chasing the dream, but I was really just chasing the bottle.

Not to say it was a complete waste of time. I did have a few accomplishments over the years. But for the most part, I was never really able to make a big enough splash to make enough money to keep at it.

So I did what every actor trying to make it in Hollywood does. I waited tables. I waited tables for far too long. And I got way too good at it. And it gave me flexibility to "follow my dreams". But really it just put me in a better position to drink more, because I was always around the booze. So at the end of every shift, the drinking would commence.

And into the wee hours, it would continue. I would either finish out the night at one of my many favorite bars, or at some party, or with friends at someone's place, or just passed out at home. And that became the daily routine. My life centered around when I was going to be drinking.

That's all my body really wanted to know too. My body just craved booze. I would get the shakes in my hands during the day. That made for a hell of a time trying to deliver martinis to tables, let me tell ya. Do you get the day shakes? If so, that's a good sign that you probably need to stop.

So basically, I became a functioning drunk. I hung out with drinkers, and we were all really good at drinking. I mean true professionals. I remember thinking it was like a job where I would clock in at cocktail hour. An eight-hour shift was common. I would drink triple vodkas with a splash of cranberry (for color), and I could finish anywhere from 5 to 8 of those a night. My friends nicknamed my drink the Joshtail. And that's how they would order it for me at the bars. "He'll take a Joshtail". And the bartenders knew exactly what that was because it was a nightly occurrence.

So depending on how much I had to eat would determine how shitfaced I would get. I'll admit that I don't remember a lot of nights. But some of the nights I do remember I wish I could forget. I've done some pretty stupid shit. I mean not like Andy Dick stupid or anything. That lunatic actually bit my ear one night at Norms diner because he thought I was making fun of him. I never got that crazy. But I may have been making fun of Andy. I don't remember.

But let's just say, I've done my share of being the drunk asshole. I won't go into details about the last night that I drank but it was pretty awful, and it was ultimately my wake-up call. Or "rock bottom" as they call it in AA.

I have nothing against AA, and I think that program has done amazing things for a lot of people. However, for me, it just didn't appeal. I had no desire to go and share my story with a bunch of strangers. I totally agree with the aspects of helping other people through their issues, but for me, it was much less complicated and time consuming than all that. I also didn't like the idea of feeling like I had a disease and that I had to stay totally sober for the rest of my life. I also believe there are incredible benefits to cannabis and psilocybin (in small doses), and that is something that AA will never get behind. Although the research shows that both weed and mushrooms help people medicinally.

I just needed to stop drinking because I was hurting myself. But more importantly, I was hurting others around me. So I woke up, and I quit. And it was the best decision I have ever made for myself. And my life has become increasingly better.

It's been an ongoing process of evolution. It took time evolving into someone who isn't an entirely selfish prick. Not someone who only cares about himself and when he is going to get drunk again. Now I've evolved into an actual human being, with feelings and a heart, and I truly care about other people. Back then I was doing absolutely nothing good for myself, or my loved ones, or the world in general. But boy was I having fun!

Now I can safely say that I'm not the same guy I used to be. I obviously still have a lot to learn, and a long way to go to get where I want to be in life. But I'm getting there with a clear conscience, and a much healthier liver.

I can't imagine what my liver must have looked like back then. It's weird to think that I had two different cousins die from liver failure from drinking too much. They were both only in their early 40's. One of them was an amazing singer, and the other one had a daughter. I didn't really know them, but I remember hearing that and thinking how that could've been me too.

This also goes without saying, but I'm going to say it anyway. We are all completely different souls on totally different paths in this lifetime. And I'm not here to tell you what you should or shouldn't do, because ultimately everything you do is your decision. I'm simply here to tell you what has been working for me and if you wanted to give these things a try, they might work for you too. I just feel the need to share now because I feel so amazing all the time and I'm a much more interesting, motivated person. As I sit here writing this, I can't help but think about how I never would've taken the time to even attempt to write a freaking book when I was drinking. I would've been too busy drinking!

With alcohol, I noticed that the more I would drink, the more I needed to drink to get drunk. So I built up this crazy tolerance. I'm not a big guy. I'm 5'9, and I weigh around 150lbs, and I was putting down enough for a few linebackers combined. The body is extraordinary like that too. It adapts to what you're doing to it. That is, for as long as the body can handle it.

The fact that my body let me consume that much on a regular basis for so many years, and I'm still here to tell the tale, is truly amazing. And I wasn't even thinking about it really being a problem. It's just how I rolled, and I'm not even sure why. For whatever reason, from deep in my subconscious mind, I sought refuge in booze.

Alcohol, sugar, pesticides, toxicants, and plastics are killing off so much on this planet, and it's a tragedy. There seems to be another agenda at play that we know nothing about. Population control is very real. It's pretty obvious that whoever is running the show, wants to keep us numb and dumb so we can't think for ourselves. Our true potential has been stifled.

If you want to fall prey to all these problems, and become another victim of the system that is trying to kill you, then join the club. I choose not to be in that club. They are trying to get rid of you after they make as much money as they possibly can off you first. Whoever "they" are.

You have to become a rebel to this system. One of the best ways to do this, is to ignore all the advertisements that are coming at you on a constant basis. You can change the way you see those billboards, or those commercials, or the nightly news. It's all designed to brainwash you. If you can rebel against all of it, you will start to raise your consciousness. That starts by going inward and getting in touch with nature. And once that begins to happen, alcohol will start to seem like just another one of those brainwashing tactics that has complete control of you.

I don't know about you, but I don't want to be controlled by these "powers that be". No thanks! They just want to get us sick by buying their poison, so we will have to buy their prescription medications. Well, I personally refuse to allow that to happen to me. As long as they keep us numb and dumb, then they can control us. Whoever "they" are.

This book is also designed to wake you up as well. As long as you are wasted, then you are not waking up. I'm here to tell you that your thought patterns and desires can change. With a few simple, small changes in your brain and in your habits, you can reverse this desire to drink. In fact, you can get to a point where you can't even imagine taking a drink again.

It's not easy to make changes in our lives. We are conditioned to repeat patterns of behavior based on what we are used to. Or what we think makes us happy. Or gives us a buzz. But that buzz eventually wears off, and we are still left with the bare essence of who we are. And if you don't know who that person is, the only way to get to know that person, is by going inward.

Meditation is the only way that I know of to do this. Without meditation in some form, you will not be able to progress to the next phase of your evolution. I can't stress enough how much meditation has helped me with every aspect of my life. We will get into that more later, as well as many other life changing habits that will make you a better you.

No one can make you change. You have to want to do it for you and you alone. I'm just here to tell you that if you are willing to make these changes in your life, then you will live a longer, happier, healthier life. Your brain will begin to heal, and you will start to think clearly.

If you are drinking now, and it's even close to the way I was going, then you will be dead, or brain dead, sooner than you need to be. And if you're still drinking too much, then it's affecting others around you too. If you actually wake up and become the person that you are capable of becoming, then you can start to help change the world for the better.

We need more people to wake up and help do some good for others. Instead of just killing ourselves with all these damn poisons that are being pushed on us. Alcohol was the primary one for me, which is just processed sugar. In case you didn't know, we have a HUGE sugar problem in this country. Alcohol and sugar are not food groups. Yet, it seems like most Americans consume more calories from these two things alone, than anything else. How does this make any sense? We are intentionally putting these poisons in our bodies that have zero nutritional value. It's all about the sugar high that your body feels, but this high is artificial.

Did you know that the human body can't excrete alcohol? It's poisonous to us, so when we take it in, the liver has to change it into acetaldehyde. What is that you ask? Well according to Suri, 'acetaldehyde is a colorless volatile liquid aldehyde obtained by oxidizing ethanol. This asks a LOT from our liver to do this critical detox work. So if the body can't do this effectively, then the acetaldehyde will accumulate which is actually what leads to hangovers from overconsumption.

This can mess with digestion utilization and absorption of nutrients. It can play havoc with sex hormone balance for both men and women. It increases body fat and decreases liver function. It dehydrates and also adds to poor sleep quality. Not to mention the social implications on relationships. It takes away from your energy and vitality and your overall greatness. Why do you need it then? Well...You don't.

So what do you think? Are you ready to make a change today? Right now, in this moment? It really is that simple. Just say it out loud to yourself and to the universe. Say "I'm ready to make a change". Go on say it! It starts right there with the decision to stop drinking. You just decide, and then you allow your brain to hear this message. Close your eyes and say it again. Now take a huge breath in and fill up your belly. Then exhale for as long as you can. Go ahead; I'll wait. Feels good right?

If you are still drinking, then your body is winning an ongoing battle with your brain. Your brain knows that you haven't been treating yourself right, but your body continues to crave these things, and wins out over the logical mind.

Well, now it's time to get your body to line up with your brain and to start working in unison. If you treat your body properly, then you will treat your brain properly too. At first, your body may fight you because it still craves all the poison you have been giving it all this time. But over time, these small changes will be easier and easier to handle, because you will feel the positive results. And once you feel how good life can be without alcohol, you will wonder why you wasted so much time and money killing yourself in the first place.

Imagine if you actually started giving your body what it needs instead of what it doesn't? What a concept! Right? But this is my goal for you. That you start to see the poison for exactly what it is, and then you start to see what healthy life choices can do to your overall wellbeing.

You may be reading this and thinking that you don't have a drinking problem. Maybe it's just a straight up sugar addiction. Or maybe it's junk food. It seems we are all addicted to something. Whatever your issue is, you can change it. It doesn't have to be taking over your life. We don't have to be prisoners of our addictions.

Now I will probably be telling you a lot of things in this book that you already know. A lot of this information is common sense so you may be thinking "Duh" a lot. Well, I used to know a lot of this info too, but when I was drinking, I just didn't do these things.

That's because I was in a self -destructive mode, and I had to transition into self- helper mode. In other words, I had to start loving myself.

So some of this information may seem dull and obvious, but I am willing to bet that if you just challenge yourself to try any of this system, your body will start to crave the good things in life instead of the bad.

Trust me when I say that you will feel so much better about everything in your life.

You will become a better you.

Now I have many stories and crazy nights that I could go into, but this book isn't about me reliving the past. This book is about you and what you need to do for yourself to get better. Once I made these decisions to better myself, I cleared out all the cobwebs in my brain and started becoming more conscious. That's why I want to share this information with you, since it has done wonders for my overall health.

So let's dig in! Shall we?

I'm reluctant to call these 'steps' because of the connection to AA, but it is really the best way to describe what we're doing here. We're taking steps toward a healthier life one self-caring act at a time. The steps can go wherever you want them to. Up, down, side to side.

These steps also don't have to be done in this order. I tried to start with the most obvious and important steps that are also the easiest to implement into your life. But if you want to jump around, feel free.

It's crazy how one act of kindness to yourself leads to another. Just like the same way that the self-destructive patterns lead to more self-destruction. It's like the body craves whatever you give it, but it either does total damage or complete good. It just depends on where your brain is in this whole process.

Why is it that we don't think of our bodies as something that requires nutrients to live? It's basic science, but we are not taught how to eat healthy here in America. Our education on food was the Basic Food Group pyramid, which has special interests in the grain, meat and dairy industries, which are heavily subsidized by the USDA. Just look at our school cafeteria meals. We all know how bad most of that food is.

I grew up in a small city in Tennessee, so the food was not healthy at all. When we are young, we just eat what's in front of us, and we don't really think about it. If no one tells us that there are actually healthier options, then we just won't know. When we eat burgers, we don't think about the fact that something had to die for us to eat that. And also, because we want to eat so many animals, the earth is pissed off.

We all know about climate change but what most people don't know is that the major reason for it is our consumption of meat. If you don't believe it, then you just aren't paying attention. And that's fine that you aren't paying attention. You aren't alone. If you are anything like I was, then you haven't given a shit because you've been too drunk to notice.

So I'm here to shed a little light on the new brain

that you are about to start developing. Because once you start taking care of yourself, you will start to care more about life, the planet, and your fellow man. And all the things that you used to not give a shit about, now become a little more important to you.

That's also because you will start to see how we are all connected. All life is connected and has its purpose. And when you notice that, life becomes precious. Also when you treat yourself right, your body thanks you and treats you right. And it allows your mind to suddenly have more space for better things in life. At least that is what happened to me.

It's as if there is all this room now for learning and loving. If you apply yourself to these steps of healthier choices, I truly think it will change your life for the better. Eventually, you just won't even want to drink anymore because your brain will heal itself, and you will start to make good healthy decisions. My goal for you is that you become as addicted to healthy choices as you were to alcohol. Ok NOW let's get started!

Step One

Drink clean fresh filtered water

Whatever your water habits have been in the past, I would be willing to bet that they were pretty lousy. Again, this is something that isn't really encouraged enough from childhood. And that's probably one of the reasons why 70% of the population is dehydrated. It's common sense yet so few people take it seriously. And if you drink a lot of alcohol, then it's highly likely that you are dehydrated more than most.

So it's time to get serious about your water intake. Just start by replacing your alcohol intake with water. It's the most important thing that you can do for your body. We are made up of 72% water for crying out loud! If we aren't drinking enough water, then our bodies can't function properly. It's just that simple. It's crazy that we aren't encouraged to have plenty of fresh filtered water all day every day.

And no, I'm not talking about bottled water. Bottled water is toxic, and we should not be consuming it. The tiny plastic particles and fluoride in those bottles are damaging. The fact that the Nestle Corporation is trying to privatize our water supply is absolutely disgusting. Their stupid plastic bottles are already doing so much damage to our planet. Clean water should be a right. And it should not be served in plastic bottles that are destroying our bodies and the planet in the process.

What you need to do is get yourself a good filter and start filling up a gallon jug at the beginning of your day. The gallon jug should be a no BPA thick plastic, or if you find aluminum or glass, then that would be best.

Whatever you choose, just get used to having it around you all day every day. Start your day by chugging as much as you possibly can. This will jump start your system, and also help to remind you to keep drinking water for the rest of the day. I've been doing this for a few years now, and I haven't even had a headache. Not even a sniffle. No stomach issues. Nothing. I honestly can't remember the last time I was sick. And that includes just general low energy. Now, as you will see there are many steps to follow that add to my wellbeing but, I truly feel like this gallon of water a day step alone, has been a huge factor as to why my body refuses to get sick.

When I was drinking booze, I never thought about water except when I would wake up in the afternoon hung over. That's when I would try to bring myself back around to some feeling of reality again. But I didn't care or even think about my water intake for the rest of the day. I would fit in a few Cokes or Mountain Dews, but then it was all about the booze when the evening kicked in. So basically 75% of my beverage intake was sugar. Processed sugar. Poison. Just pumping it into my bloodstream on a daily basis and not thinking twice about it. My body was addicted, and my brain didn't even seem to register it. So once I made the decision to stop drinking alcohol, I suddenly realized how stupid I was being to my body by not giving it enough clean water.

And it must be cleanly filtered water folks. Unless you have the money for a high-tech water filter system that gets checked regularly, then the filter I recommend is called Zerowater. It comes with a digital tester that lets you see the difference from the water before you put it through the filter and after. When it comes out 0.00 on the tester, then you know it's good to go. The filter needs to be changed when it reads 0.06 or higher. The water coming from my tap in Tennessee registers at 0.46, but then after the filter, it reads 0.00. So you can test it yourself and see the results right then. That's why I recommend this filter. The water tastes great after it's filtered through a Zerowater filter too. But if you can afford a reverse osmosis system, I hear those are best for getting everything out.

Another great habit I got into was adding organic lemon essential oils to my water. It's a great thing to add some citrus to give your water a big boost of nutrients and flavor, but it's not totally necessary. I also like to add a few drops of peppermint essential oil, and that tastes great too.

You will have a pretty difficult time drinking a ton of alcohol if you are consuming a gallon of water a day. Trust me. It's hard enough to finish a gallon of water when that's pretty much all you drink.

I always have my water bottle in arms reach. It is my lifeline. Remember we are 72% water. And when your water jug is in site, this reminds you to drink it. It also allows you to take inventory of how much you are drinking throughout your day. This is not easy to do but it's totally worth the challenge. If you stop reading this book and do this step alone and none of the other steps, I believe that you will see a significant boost to your overall health and wellbeing.

Here's an amazing thing about water. It holds onto memories and it can absorb energy. So if you send healing positive energy into your water, it will react to those thoughts. Be sure to think about that while you drink your water too.

Once you make this first healthy choice, then you're on the fast train to recovery. As I mentioned before, one healthy choice leads to another. So I am certain that if you get into this habit first, you will see great changes that will lead to more changes too. So once you stop chugging the booze, then you can start chugging the water.

Step 2

Go to SLEEP!!!

Sorry, I shouldn't have yelled that since I'm trying to get you to go to sleep. Ok, I'm going to whisper it now. Go to sleeeeeeeeep. Seriously. You have been destroying your body for a long time now, and your body needs to heal itself. You have also been messing up your sleep patterns with all the booze. It's time to train your body to get seven to nine good hours of uninterrupted sleep. Every night.

I know it's difficult. Getting enough sleep is probably one of the hardest things for us to do in this day and age. Especially with all the blue screens everywhere. It's very hard for me to go to bed early. I've been a night owl my whole life. But now with the computers and the TVs, it's just so hard to make myself get to bed early. However, if I go to bed late I will still make sure I'm getting at least 7 hours of sleep. It's so important! It's been said that sleep is more important than food.

This is how we heal and recover. So if you skip this crucial health choice, then you are not helping yourself. You can actually cause brain damage by not getting enough sleep. Not that you haven't already been doing an enormous amount of brain damage from the booze. But just think about the fact that your sleep cycle has been completely out of whack because of the booze too. So now it's time to sleep and heal.

Alcohol initially can serve as a stimulant, and then it flips and serves as a central nervous system depressant. So it can sometimes help people fall asleep, but then it will wake them up once they are into the sleep cycle. Alcohol tends to throw off circadian rhythms and disrupts sleep in our first REM cycle at night.

Alcohol not only interferes with sleep, but also our dreams. Dreams are incredibly important! According to the sleep specialist Dr. Rubin Naiman, dreams are critical for information processing, assimilation, memory, learning, and emotional healing. He also says that it's the single most overlooked factor in clinical depression. And it suppresses creativity. Look up, Dr. Rubin Naiman. He is an expert.

There is a spiritual aspect to sleep too and needs to be considered in this way. Even the Dalai Lama once said, "sleep is the best meditation". We have three levels of consciousness. 1. Waking 2. Sleeping 3. Dreaming. If we aren't paying attention to the importance of sleep, then how can we even begin to understand our dreams?

Sleep is serenity. Sleep is spirituality. Sleep is healing. Short sleepers are at risk for infection, obesity, diabetes, cancer, arthritis, mood disorders, and so on and so on. I feel like I never really learned this growing up. This information is critical to our health. And if we don't give ourselves this daily dose of sleep, then we are actually hurting ourselves.

Caffeine is a sleep disrupter. If you drink a lot of coffee, just see step 1. Replace the coffee with water. You will actually have more energy from the water. Or if you can't give up your coffee, just drink less. Some coffee can have health benefits, but the effects on your adrenal glands are not great if you drink too much. Your sleep is more important than that caffeine rush.

Over 70 million people suffer from insomnia. That's a huge number! So try not to put yourself in this category. Train yourself to sleep. Now that you are removing alcohol from the equation, it will be so much easier. And just think about all the extra time you will have to get some good sleep.

If you don't usually remember your dreams, they will start to reveal themselves to you soon. And if you remember your dreams, then this is a good sign that you got yourself to the level of sleep that you needed. REM deprivation results in fatigue and depression as well.

I would also recommend taking all the blue screens out of your room when you sleep. Those EMF waves are not helping your sleep at all. And if you use the alarm on your phone, then at least set it to airplane mode, so it's not sending out the waves while you sleep. I started taking my phone out of my room at night, and my sleep improved a lot.

Another thing I would recommend is using essential oils in a diffuser for your sleep time. Look into the benefits of essential oils, and you will be amazed. I have become obsessed with them, and I love the aroma that they give off too. Organixx is an awesome organic brand that is reasonably priced. It only requires a few drops at a time, and the smells of lavender, eucalyptus, peppermint, clove, rosemary, grapefruit, or geranium rose, etc. will only add to your dreams.

If you apply this simple step of sleeping, the benefits will be truly amazing. It's just plain science. The better you sleep, the better you will feel.

So now that you are drinking water and sleeping better, you are well on your way to recovery and healing. If you stop reading right now and only did these two steps, you would see huge results in your health. It's also not going to be as easy to go get wasted if you are feeling these benefits. So get some good sleep. Sweet dreams!

Step 3

Look at the reasons why you drink

In order to get to the core of the problem, we need to address the cause and rewire the brain. Whatever happened to you as a child that has caused you to drink so much is behind you now. You can choose to let it define who you are, or you can choose to beat the addiction.

You have a sugar addiction. Most Americans are addicted to sugar in one way or another. Sugar is the devil. You have chosen to get your sugar in a much larger dose with alcohol. So we need to get you off of this alcohol sugar and ideally get you off of all processed sugar. Sugar is the devil but has everyone convinced that it's not. Watch the documentary "Sugar Coated" if you need some encouragement. It's extremely enlightening. Sugar is the problem. It's common for alcoholics to stop drinking and replace the alcohol with another form of the same sugar addiction. So you will want to avoid the doughnuts and soda and junk food.

Don't freak out because there are other forms of sugar that are natural and delicious that will become very good friends in the near future. Fruit, honey, stevia, and maple syrup are a few.

3.3 Million people die every year from alcohol related causes. 80% to 90% of alcoholics don't seek treatment, and of those 10% that do seek treatment, 90% of those people relapse in the first 4 years. Really? That's insane! Why is it so hard to quit and stay quit? A person dies every 10 seconds from Alcohol Use Disorder or AUD. How are we still so hard wired to continue down this path of destruction? It appears the addiction is in control. The body overrides the brain and logic seems to go out the window.

Even if the brain knows how wrong it is, the body still continues to drink more and more. It's a habit. I don't personally think it's a disease like AA claims. I think it's a choice. It's not all genetic either. Genes only mean we are prone to certain things, but we don't have to allow the genes to win out. We can fight anything we want. Our brains are incredibly powerful, and our thoughts can heal. This is yet another thing that we are not taught when we are young, and we should be.

So if you start to pay attention to these reasons why you drink, then I think you will also start to notice how obsessed our society is with alcohol.

Society is the number one pusher of booze. It's almost impossible to avoid being advertised to in some way. More money is spent on beer commercials than anything. We are encouraged by friends, family, peers, TV and films, advertisements, and especially at restaurants or bars when we go out to eat. It has become interwoven into our subconscious from childhood. No matter what your exposure is to alcohol, you will come in contact with it in one way or another at a very young age.

I feel like there should be a class taught on how

to ignore advertisements. We have to make a conscious effort to ignore all of it. I personally can't stand hearing any commercials of any kind. It's like nails on a chalkboard to me. I just don't like the feeling of being sold to against my will. If I'm ever watching network TV or listening to the radio and a commercial comes on, I will turn that station or change that channel so fast. I used to audition for commercials when I was acting, but it always felt weird to want to sell someone else's product with my face. That's probably why I didn't book very many.

There is a lot of money being spent on keeping us numb and dumb. The more we pay into the system, the more we are asking to remain numb and dumb. Billions of dollars a year are being spent on keeping our veins pumped with this poison. It flows into everything from our food, to our booze, and even our soil. There is nothing good that can come from buying into this system.

This is why we must become rebels. We must rebel from the poison. If you want to avoid being a sheep, then don't buy what they are selling to the sheep. If you do, then you are paying to let them kill you. Think about that for a second. Do you want to live a good, long, healthy life? Then avoid the machine. Avoid the pharmaceuticals, the processed GMO foods, the sugar, but most importantly, the alcohol.

Once you do this and begin to treat yourself right, and eat the foods that come straight from the earth, you will start to wake up. All of these poisons will start to seem evil. And that's because they are evil. And they are meant to keep you controlled.

Learn how to reject these poisons and see them for what they really are. I mean seriously, is there any logic to allowing booze to pickle your liver? Is there any logic to allowing this substance to ruin your life? At first, it's usually about fitting in. I get that. We all start out trying it because we aren't supposed to. I guess if you tell someone they can't have something then they will just want it more. Often it's a pattern that's learned from our elders, and this behavior needs to be corrected.

That's why these kids are tempted to drink so young here in America. In other countries like Italy, it's not looked at as being so bad for younger kids. So it doesn't become this forbidden fruit where kids are going out of their way to get it. Wine especially is just part of their culture and the kids don't abuse it like they do here in the US.

So this step is all about just paying attention to the reasons that you drink. Pay attention to the deep, dark reasons within yourself, but also the exterior reasons that are unavoidable. We must correct the "drinking thinking".

Step 4

Learn how to meditate

I'm willing to bet that if you are a heavy drinker, then you have probably never really meditated. Or at least if you have, then it's not something that has become a practice. Well, I'm here to tell you that meditation will change your life for the better in every way imaginable. This is science people! Look into it.

Many people have some weird view of what meditation is, or they just think it's some kind of hippie thing. Certain religions will tell you it's evil, but they are telling you that because they don't want you to challenge their religion.

Meditation is not anti-religion. It gets you in touch with your true divine self. It's a very spiritual experience to go inward. It may cause you to start thinking for yourself, and this is why it can be threatening to some religions. Meditation has become the single most important spiritual practice that I follow. It has become an everyday routine that I can't imagine doing without now.

There are probably thousands of different types of meditation out there, so you may need to do your own research. I practice two different types of meditation. The first and main one that I practice is called Transcendental Meditation or TM. This is the practice that became popular through The Beatles here in America in the 60's. Maharishi Mahesh Yogi brought it here, and TM has since become very popular among many other creative types. David Lynch, Jerry Seinfeld, Russell Brand, Dr. Oz, Deepak Chopra, Russell Simmons, Heather Graham, Katy Perry, Ellen DeGeneres, Hugh Jackman, Etc. The list of successful people that do TM is huge.

This is not necessarily a reason to do this practice, but you have to notice the trend here. People that do TM usually have their shit together. However, what TM can do for you, goes way beyond getting your shit together. It helps reduce blood pressure. It helps with anxiety, depression, anger, PTSD, insomnia, ADHD, addiction and just overall stress. It is absolutely effortless, and it is proven effective.

Now, do you see why I have put this step so close to the top? It helps with everything, but especially addiction. It reduces your cortisol levels lower than when you sleep. If you don't know about cortisol, it's the stress hormone. It's the fight or flight hormone that can wreak havoc on your body when it's out of whack. Which, if you've been heavily drinking for a long time, then your entire system is out of whack. You need to learn to control and balance your mind, and this is the fastest, safest way to do that. TM reduces the desire to get angry or upset, which therefore decreases the desire to drink.

Another great thing about TM is that it's meant to be practiced twice a day. Twenty minutes in the morning and twenty minutes in the evening. It's an amazing escape that becomes like a sanctuary. It also helps the creative mind to flourish, which also keeps the mind off of drinking.

You will be amazed at how dramatically this will affect everything in your life. Go check out (www. TM.ORG) if you want more information. TM has done wonders for kids in school, prisoners in jail, and people with PTSD. There is, unfortunately, a fee to learn from the foundation, but it's the best way to learn the practice and to get it into your body. It is effortless and can be learned in just a few days. If you can't afford it, they have scholarship plans. If you still can't afford it, then you can find your mantra on line and start doing it on your own. However, this is not recommended to get the full effects of the practice, but it is still better than not doing it at all.

The other meditation technique that I practice is called Twin Hearts Meditation. It is extremely powerful.

It should be paired with an energy healing practice called Pranic Healing. However, the meditation alone can be used for self-healing or for the maintenance of good health.

Pranic Healing is a learned energy healing technique that everyone has the ability to do, but it does require a course. It is highly effective for helping to clear out chakras and to heal the body. The Twin Hearts Meditation can be done without learning Pranic Healing, but this may be something that interests you in the future. I believe that this healing energy can do wonders for people going through addiction withdrawals. It will also just help with overall wellbeing.

You may want to seek out a Pranic Healer to do some healing on you, and if you are in a big city, there is probably someone nearby. But if you are just interested in the Twin Hearts Meditation, then it is a guided meditation where you just listen to the healing voice of Master Choa Kok Sui and follow his instructions. It involves blessing the earth and everything in it, a series of OMs, and picturing a healing white light entering your crown chakra and going through every part of your body. It's awesome, and I do feel like this meditation brings positive results. However, this may be a bit more advanced and time consuming for a brand-new meditator. If you would like more information on Pranic Healing, check out (www.pranichealingcenter.com). Google chakras if you need more basic information on this.

But as I mentioned before, there are many different types of meditation, and it will just help you to get into it now. Whichever methods you choose, just do yourself a favor and implement this habit into your life. It will be the best thing you can do for your health and dealing with your addiction. It will also be the best way to start the momentum for more healthy choices.

If you are anxious to get started, there is an app called "Insight Timer" which is great for tracking your meditation progress. It also has many other different guided meditations that you can get started with right away. Start with a five-minute meditation if you aren't ready to jump into the longer ones yet. Just start meditating in some fashion. It will change your life.

There is a book out now called "10% Happier" by Dan Harris that is all about how meditation will help make you a ten percent happier person. I think it's actually more than that.

It's also been said that if every child in the world learned how to meditate at the age of eight, then we would have world peace in one lifetime. That's only eighty years! I say we make this part of our education system and watch what happens to the future generations.

Step 5

Detox with a liver cleanse

You need to reset your entire system but mostly your liver. One of the best ways to do that is to cleanse all the toxicants that you have been accumulating over the years. Now you'll probably want to do some research to see which one works for you. There is one called a True Cellular Detox that I have been hearing about lately. It sounds like a great way to go if you want to go big. It's expensive and time consuming though. For me, I started to detox with juice.

What I recommend is watching the documentary "Fat, Sick and Nearly Dead" and consider doing a juice cleanse. This documentary will have a powerful effect on you. It certainly did for me. At the time when I watched it, I had never really considered getting my nutrients from fruits and veggies. It seems like common sense to me now, but then it was like this huge epiphany.

Also, the guy who made the movie was so much worse off than I was. I was just a drunk. But this guy was overweight, loaded up on pills and steroids, and had a debilitating autoimmune disease. He traded in the booze and junk food and completely transformed his life in 60 days. It's an amazing story, and Joe Cross is very entertaining. He is also completely inspirational, and even if you aren't overweight, you still see the importance of getting your nutrients primarily from vegetables and fruit.

This struck a chord with me for some reason, and I started thinking about how few vegetables I had in my life. And fruit? I love fruit, and I just didn't seek it out before. I wasn't thinking about it because I was too busy destroying my body instead of taking care of it.

So I went out and got myself the same juicer he used in the documentary. The Breville cost a couple of hundred dollars, but I had been saving money since I quit drinking. And you will too. So I was willing to invest this in myself and I started juicing like crazy. I was making three or four juices a day at first. I was nuts about my juicer.

All of sudden I'm getting all these greens that I never thought about before. And beets, and carrots, and ginger, and apples, and pineapple, and kale, YES kale, and swiss chard, and parsley, and so on and so on. I was still eating food as well, but it started making me think differently about all my food choices. Since I started getting all these nutrients from nature, and I was touching the food and caring for it too, I felt more connected to the earth.

I also felt less of a connection to meat and wasn't

craving it as much. So this step ultimately led me to becoming a "mostly vegan" as I call it. You may not find this happens for you. But, if you start juicing like I did, you will start to change your appreciation for your food and where it comes from.

I started to notice how juicing was such a great way to get my vitamins. It also helped with the sugar cravings since now I was able to take in natural sugar from the juice. Since alcohol is just sugar, this was a nice treat for me to have fruit juice.

This will start to alter your mindset towards getting the right type of sugar. Ultimately, it's a good idea to do more veggies than fruit because fruit is still sugar, but you can taper off the amount of fruit you add to your juices, and they will still taste great. You may have an issue with taste on the veggie juices, but this is the beauty of juicing, you can add fruit or ginger or mint to mask the flavor at first. Eventually, your palette will change, and you will actually crave these veggie juices too.

A general rule is if it comes from nature and it's edible, then it's most likely great for you. If it's processed then beware. I'm not going to guide you on any specific diet, because most diets don't really work long term. However, we can all agree that eating more fruits and vegetables is wise. Some people need to avoid all sugar, but fruit is nature's candy and is still beneficial for most.

So if you are anything like Joe Cross and countless others who are overweight, then you will probably start to lose weight on this cleanse as well. Along with steps 1-4, it is highly likely that you will see a drop in your weight. And that probably won't be a bad thing. Even if you're a beanpole and don't need to lose any weight, it's still wise to eat your fruits and veggies. But you already know that. Right?

Also, you want to make sure that you are eating organic produce. This is VERY important. You do not want to be putting pesticides or GMOs in your body. Glyphosate is the main pesticide in Roundup, which is sprayed on everything. It is toxic and needs to be avoided at all costs. If the cost of going organic is an issue, then just do it anyway. You are paying for peace of mind. It will still be cheaper than going to the hospital. Look for that USDA organic or Non-GMO symbol.

I like to think of myself as a conscious rebel. I personally rebel against anything that big business is encouraging us to consume. Unfortunately, you just can't trust most of it. Ideally, in a perfect world, you would grow your own organic produce. But obviously, that's not easy for most of us. If you can get in touch with a local farm, or hit up your farmers market to get as close to the source as you can. That's the best-case scenario.

I was so surprised by how tasty these juices were too. Let's be honest, did you ever really enjoy the taste of alcohol? How many shots did you do that made you want to vomit? Why not think of doing a straight shot of ginger instead? It will give you the same burning sensation you used to get when doing a shot of tequila. Except it's actually good for you instead of poison for you. You won't get that drunk buzz after, but it's going to give you a natural buzz. Which is so much better in the long run.

And if you can handle a shot of tequila, then you can handle a shot of wheatgrass. So stop whining about the taste and just drink it because it's good for you.

Start experimenting with juice and eventually you will start to get addicted to it. The human body is an incredible biocomputer. It craves what you give it. So you will start to crave the healthy juices if you give your body these amazing gifts from nature.

And don't get confused by many of the juices you see in the store. Some of them are okay, but most of them have added sugar. Cartons of orange juice, for example, are made with many oranges and can spike your blood sugar. It's best to just juice your own. It tastes so much better to get it right from the orange anyway.

Cold pressed juices are apparently the best way to get the most nutrients out of your produce. If you are using the fast spinning juicers, that's fine for now, but eventually, you will want to upgrade to the best you can get.

There is a new reasonably priced cold pressed juicer on the market that I haven't tried yet, but it's the one I would buy today if I were just starting out. It's called the Hurom, and it looks awesome. The cleanup is supposed to be much easier too.

If you have the money and want to buy a whole detox juice program from one of the organic, cold pressed juiceries in your neighborhood; then you can do that too. Just make sure they are organic. Look carefully though, because they are not easy to find. Even in the big cities. Which is another reason why it's best to do it on your own. But if you have the money and don't have the time to do it yourself, then buy them pre-done. Glass bottles are best.

In LA there is an awesome grocery store called Erewhon. It's a bit pricey, but they are all organic. There are a few other places out there that are great too, but you may not be near them. So wherever you are, find organic juice. It won't be cheap, unfortunately. A good organic, fresh cold pressed juice can cost you about 8 to 10 bucks each, depending on where you go. Hey, it's still less than a cocktail at a club. Right? If you want to save time and money, there are some quality green powders that have tons of nutrients. Organixx also has an awesome green powder that is apparently 33 times more potent than juicing. It's not cheap either so unfortunately we have to pay through the nose for it. Actually, you pay through the whole body. You are worth it tho and your body will thank you for it too.

Step 6

Immerse yourself in nature

Most people are deficient in Vitamin D. This is a huge health problem. Guess where we get Vitamin D? Obviously from the sun! So go for a hike. A run. A jog. A walk. Stand with your bare feet on the ground for at least three minutes a day. This is called grounding, and it is miraculous. Grounding can do wonders for inflammation. This is science people! So just go outside!

It actually lowers blood flow to the pre-frontal cortex, and the amygdala in the brain. When this happens, it causes you to slow down the thinking part of the brain that makes you want to drink in the first place. And when you lower the blood flow to the amygdala, this is the part deep inside the emotional brain, that's when you can get more in touch with yourself.

I don't know about you, but I can't think of too many times that I would drink and go for a hike. It just doesn't really make sense to the mind, body, and earth connection. When you are outside, especially in the woods, you are receiving prana or energy from the trees. If you actually put your hands on the tree or hug it, you will get energy from that tree. And then you will be a 'tree hugger' too. This is a good thing. All those 'tree huggers' you have been making fun of are just more aware than you. But you are getting closer. If you have applied steps 1-5, then this just makes sense as the next logical healing step.

Also, because you are getting more in touch with you, nature is the best place to go deeper. When you lose yourself in the entertainment of all the life that surrounds you, it is such a joy. Meditation outside is always great to do too.

I've seen some incredible things in nature, and I have barely seen anything in the grand scope of the earth. I have actually seen trees that have made me laugh. When I'm on nature walks, random animals like deer or turtles or butterflies, will show up just for me to view. It feels like such a treat to discover new life that you may not have ever taken the time to notice before. Just be in the moment and appreciate all that life has to offer you. Because when you stop to think about it, everything in this life is an absolute miracle. You, being alive in this moment, at this time on earth, is nothing short of miraculous. Embrace that thought.

When I was drinking, I never thought about that fact. You can't have these experiences inside a bar. The idea of going to do outdoor activities was far from my mind back then. Unless it was about going to a music festival, then I was all about it. Actually, I am still very much into outdoor music festivals, but I will get into that in a later step.

I'm just saying that enjoying the outdoors does not usually make you want to drink. So get your ass outside and breathe in nature. It's scientific medicine for your brain and your overall wellbeing. Oh, and if you aren't getting enough Vitamin D from the sun, you should be taking a supplement. But the sun is much more effective, and quite a bit cheaper too.

Step 7

Exercise Exercise Exercise

I say this one three times because it's that important. You know this is something you need to do, but most likely you aren't doing it. Or if you are, then you are probably not getting great results because of your booze belly.

For me, it was a vodka gut. I used to be 'skinny fat' when I was drinking. But I would still work out through my hangovers. I would go sweat out the booze so I could turn around and do it all over again later that night. Not the best routine, but I was in LA and thought I needed to be at the gym. Although now I look more in shape than I ever did when I was working out four or five days a week. Lately, I've just been doing pushups and yoga, and that has been working for me for now.

Maybe you're one of those people who can stay motivated to go to the gym even through the booze. And that's great if you can manage to do that. Apparently, even if you drink a lot, working out can considerably lower the risks of major damage. The problem there is not many people want to work out when they are in the self-destructive mode and trying to recover from over consumption. Most drinkers I was around were not big fans of working out. Except to do twelve-ounce curls to the face.

So here is the thing with working out. You don't have to go crazy. You don't even need to join a gym. All you have to do is motivate yourself to do something active. Everyday. And if you can't fit it in everyday, then at least 30 minutes 3 times a week. You may not need to do a bunch of cardio and weight training. You may need to do more relaxing Tai Chi or yoga type movements. Listen to your body and do what feels right for you. Start slow if you haven't worked out much before. This is crucial. Don't hurt yourself.

If this is new for you, then just start by going for walks and then ease into the jog, if that's what feels good. Start with pushups. Just do as many as you can, even if it's 10 a day. After a few days, you can raise that to 20 a day. The next thing you know, you will be busting out 100 and not even thinking about it.

It's all about getting your body into the habit of being active. Don't beat yourself up trying to get in perfect shape. Just be proud of yourself for choosing to take the healthy path. Even if it takes some time getting there, you are doing it, and that's what counts.

You can also combine step 6 with this step too and go outside to exercise. I like to do pushups in the grass sometimes because I can get that extra prana from the earth.

I'm sure that you probably know many benefits of exercise, but let me just remind you of a few. Exercise can prevent, control and even reverse diabetes. It can have a positive impact on mood, blood pressure, depression, stress and of course body weight. In fact, exercise will have a positive effect on every aspect of your life. There is no medical condition that can't be improved by physical exercise.

So get off your ass and start doing something physical! You are going to need a place to put all that drinking energy you used to put out there. Now you can put that energy into helping yourself instead of hurting yourself. It doesn't take long at all to see results too. A friend of mine just posted a shirtless before and after shot of himself on Facebook today, and the results were amazing. In eleven months he went from being very out of shape to being very in shape. So if you need motivation, check out some before and after pictures. You can completely change your body in less than a year if you really try.

You are already doing all these great things since you started the first 6 steps. Right? Why not just do the next most obvious positive health choice? And if you already exercise, just keep it up. Now that you quit drinking, exercise will help your body heal itself even faster. So get moving!

Step 8

Write

Start a journal or a diary. OK, maybe this sounds a little trite to you. You can call it whatever you want, but just write. Hand-write on actual paper. You need a place to put all those thoughts in your over thinking head. Drinkers are often over thinkers.

I've known some of the most brilliant minds that can drink like fish. Over thinking was common amongst my drinking buddies. Me included. I know I was in my head a lot more when I was drinking. Maybe it was because I had to work twice as hard to think through the drunk brain. Or maybe I just needed to slow down the thoughts and drinking helped with that. Thankfully now my mind is much more centered.

I used to watch these brilliant brains turn to

mush after a few cocktails. The conversations became increasingly less intelligent as the night progressed. Of course, in our heads, we were becoming more intelligent. When you aren't drinking, start listening to 'drunk talk' if you find yourself around it. Now ask yourself... do these people sound smart? Guess what? You sounded just like that and probably even worse. But I digress.

Writing is an incredible way to get these thoughts out. And the best way to do this is at the beginning of your day. If you do it this way, it's called 'morning pages' by the author Julia Cameron. Her book "The Artist's Way: A Spiritual Path To Higher Creativity" is a self-help book that helps people with artistic creative recovery. It is on the list of the Top 100 Best Self-Help Books of All Time. It's an awesome 12-week course that helps bring out your inner creative child. Julia says, "God is an artist. So are we. And we can cooperate with each other. Our creative dreams and longings do come from a divine source, not from the human ego.«

The morning pages are one of the biggest commitments of the program, but it is very helpful. You basically just free form hand-write whatever is on your mind for three pages. You write till you hit three pages and then you stop. You don't read back over it; you just move on with your day. It's very beneficial, and it really helps to clear out the cobwebs in the brain. You will find that it helps you to focus those thoughts. Then once they are on paper, they sort of leave your brain. You don't need to harp on the thoughts because you got them out of your head and on paper. It's pretty great. The first day I did it, I was inspired to write a song. So I noticed the effects immediately.

If you are feeling creatively stuck, The Artist's Way is an awesome way to help with this. An ex-girlfriend of mine claims that doing The Artist's Way is what helped her get sober. It just causes you to do a lot of introspective work, and makes you take a look at your true self. This may be scary for some, but I found it to be quite liberating. It's a great way to tap into that youthful artist within you.

Everyone is an artist in some way. We are all creative beings, and when we are creating, it puts us closest to our creator. So whether or not you do these morning pages, just try to start writing in a notebook. Anytime you want to get some thoughts out. It doesn't have to be in the morning; it's just good to get it all out at the beginning of your day, so you don't have to let those thoughts fester later. But really anytime you feel like you need to work through something, you should just write.

Step 9

Eat healthier

Cooking at home is the healthiest way to eat. It takes a little extra time, but it's worth it. You can actually feel and taste the energy and the love you are putting into your food. This is far better than eating out and not knowing who is cooking your food, or where the food is coming from. Preparing your food also gives your body time to prepare itself for the food you are about to put inside you. This is obviously better for you than grabbing fast food and not giving your body time to prepare itself. We just want to avoid the fast food mentality that so many Americans have become accustomed to.

Eating healthier will probably start to happen naturally as a result of the juicing. Now that you are familiar with eating organic produce, you are already half way there. Just keep going with it and throw the net out wider. Eating whole organic foods is like breast-feeding from the earth herself. Eat for your health not just for flavor. Although eating healthy can also be delicious too believe it or not. If you don't already, it's time to start cooking at home.

This way you can cook with the safest best fats like coconut or avocado oil. Coconut oil is a natural miracle that I became familiar with a few years ago, and I swear by it. There are incredible benefits to coconut oil, and I use it all the time for everything. This may sound crazy, but 'oil pulling' is great for balancing the bacteria in your mouth. We will get into mouth health and oil pulling more later. This is a great habit to get into, but it takes about fifteen to twenty minutes so you may need to multi-task. Writing is always a good thing to do while oil pulling. Here's another way to combine steps! Just make sure you spit it out before you reach the 20-minute mark. If you don't, then the toxins you just pulled from your mouth will start to get into your bloodstream. Just don't spit in the toilet or down the sink, so you don't clog your plumbing. Then brush your teeth (with a non-fluoride toothpaste).

Coconut oil has medium chain triglycerides (MCTs) and is even great for early onset Alzheimer's. Just eating big scoops of it can slow down this process. Alzheimer's is a scary disease that is destroying way too many lives. This must change! If you keep drinking excessively, then it's very likely that you will see some dementia in your old age. Wouldn't you rather have quality years at the end of your life? I certainly would.

Coconut oil is also great for infection in the throat, and it also gives you energy too. It is one of the healthiest fats you can consume. However, avocados are probably the best source of healthy fats. When you cook with coconut oil, it also keeps its nutrients even after it's heated. So it's totally unique to other oils.

I'm not going to get into what you should or shouldn't be eating. One person's food is another person's poison. So whether or not you choose to eat meat is up to you. I have chosen not to consume any meat other than fish on occasion, but that's just me. If you choose to eat meat just make sure it is organic. Make sure all your food is organic if possible. There are a few things that you can get away with that don't matter as much. Check out the list of the Dirty Dozen or the Clean Fifteen online to get a better idea of this.

We all know the phrase about breakfast being the most important meal of the day. Well, this is probably true, but we need to start making this meal healthy. One of the things that I'm habitual about is my morning smoothie. I call it the 'perfect smoothie', and I use a Nutribullet 900 series to make it. I have used this almost daily for the last few years. The reason I started with the smoothie was to make sure I was getting my greens everyday. It's been easier for me to get it out of the way first thing in the morning.

Let's be honest, we all know we need to eat greens. But who has time to eat a bunch of kale or broccoli? When I realized I could just mix my greens into a smoothie and I would barley taste them, I was hooked. Now it's a daily regimen.

My 'perfect smoothie' consists of mostly greens. I will fill the biggest cup with 3/4 organic kale, organic broccoli or organic spinach. Then I will add frozen organic blueberries, banana, ground up flax seeds, hemp seeds, chia seeds, cocoa powder, spirulina, chlorella, goji berry powder, ground up nuts, turmeric, bone broth powder, cinnamon, and then I finish it off with Açai juice. Sometimes I will use organic apple juice or some other organic green juice. It changes all the time, but it always has plenty of superfoods.

I have been drinking a perfect smoothie everyday for years along with all my other healthy choices, and I don't ever get tired of it. It fills me up for most of the afternoon, and it gives me tons of energy. It also gives me peace of mind because I'm getting my daily greens and berries and seeds. It also tastes great, and I haven't been sick a single day since I have started this. Give your own perfect smoothie a try. They are incredibly delicious. I honestly feel like if you start with just the morning smoothie, with all those greens, you will see a big boost in your health.

I'm also a big fan of quinoa and beans with avocado and veggies for a second or third meal of the day. It's quick and easy and has tons of fiber and protein. I usually spice it up with turmeric, black pepper, cayenne pepper, and cinnamon. This gives it a little spicy kick and those spices are all great for you. Turmeric is especially great for inflammation, and I suggest using it whenever possible.

And I must mention mushrooms. Eating mushrooms everyday gives your immune system quite a boost. There are some great mushroom supplements to help with this since it's not easy to get mushrooms all the time. I use a supplement from Organixx called 7M that has seven different types. Mushrooms are one of the most fascinating things on the planet, and it is worth looking into all the amazing benefits that come from them. Not just for our bodies, but for the planet too. Mushrooms are considered the Internet of the earth. It only makes sense that we should be consuming them regularly.

If you are going to use sugar for any reason try to use the healthier options. Stevia has many benefits. Or pure local unfiltered honey. Honey is considered the most spiritual food we can eat. Obviously, you don't want to overdo it, but if you eat local honey, you can adapt to most allergies in your area. There are entirely too many honey varieties on the market that should not be consumed. Many of them are not real honey. Go local. Ideally, you want the bees to come from within ten to twenty miles. If you haven't heard, the bees are in danger right now, so get that local honey while you still can.

When you start to cook at home, you will feel better just from the act of doing it yourself. This should also encourage you to avoid packaged processed foods. The more you start to get closer to the earth source for your food, the more you will realize how bad all that other junk food is. We have all become way too accepting of the processed garbage that is on every other corner of every grocery store shelf in America. It's time to adjust your view on this. Most of this processed crap is not real food. How are we supposed to thrive if we are not eating real food?

Explore and see what happens for you. If you start to try new things, you will be amazed at how many delicious, healthy foods are out there. It's really exciting when you discover new foods that are healthy and taste great. It's pretty addictive too actually. A good rule of thumb is that if you can't pronounce any ingredients on a package, then you probably should avoid it. Three or less items listed that you recognize is safest. When you look on a package of almonds, the ingredients should just read almonds. That is a safe bet.

I wouldn't recommend any fad diets though.

There is a huge misconception that diets work. They don't work. Don't believe the hype. Many people may get results from certain diets in the short term. This doesn't mean it's going to last. If you apply all of the other steps in this book, then you won't need to do some crazy diet. Just avoid all that diet nonsense and eat healthier.

Focus on veggies, plant-based proteins, beans, whole grains, and nuts. These foods are found in all the healthy blue zone areas where people live well into the hundreds. Those people eat little to no meat. I'm not suggesting you become a vegan, but eating less meat will help to elongate your life.

Step 10

Take salt showers
(Or ocean dips if you live next to the ocean)

This one may sound a bit strange. If you don't know this already, we all have a chakra system that makes up our aura. You can't see it, but it's there. The chakras can get clogged up with dirty energy, and one way to keep them clean is with salt water. The ocean is the best way to cleanse our chakras, but most of us don't live next to the ocean so salt showers can do the trick instead.

I learned much of this information from the book "Miracles Through Pranic Healing" by Master Choa Kok Sui. "It has been clairvoyantly observed that water is capable of absorbing dirty energy and salt breaks down the dirty energy".

I use sea salt, but you can use any kind of cheap iodized salt. What you want to do is step out of the water flow when you are in the shower. Put a nice sized pour of salt in your hand and begin to caress your chakras in a circular motion. Start with your Crown Chakra on the top of your head. As you make the circles repeat "Let Go" over and over. The Crown Chakra controls the pineal gland, the brain, and the entire body.

Then move to your Ajna Chakra, which is located between the eyebrows. This is also called the Master Chakra because it directs and controls the other major chakras and their corresponding endocrine glands and vital organs. It also affects the eyes and the nose. Continue chanting "Let Go" as you make a salt circle on your Ajna Chakra.

Move down to your Throat Chakra next and make a salt circle. It is located at the center of your throat. It controls and energizes the throat, the thyroid glands, parathyroid glands, and the lymphatic system. This is obviously the area where your voice comes from, so listen to it as you repeat "Let Go".

Next is your Heart Chakra. Continue with more salt and make the circles on and around your heart in the center qf your chest. This chakra energizes and controls the heart, the thymus gland, and the circulatory system.

It is closely connected to the front Solar Plexus Chakra by several big energy channels. Continue to chant "Let Go".

Then you want to move on down to the front Solar Plexus Chakra, which is located in the hollow area between the ribs. This one is major, and any congested energy needs to be cleared from here as much as possible. There is also a back Solar Plexus Chakra directly behind the front. This chakra controls and energizes the diaphragm, pancreas, liver, stomach, and to a certain degree, energizes the large and small intestines, appendix, lungs, heart and other parts of the body. This chakra also affects the quality of the blood because it controls and energizes the liver, which detoxifies the blood. So the Solar Plexus Chakra is the energy clearinghouse center, and the whole body can be energized through it. Continue to chant "Let Go" as you rub salt in a circle on your front and back Solar Plexus Chakras.

Next is your Navel Chakra. Located on the navel, it controls and energizes the small intestine, large intestine, and appendix. It affects the general vitality of a person. "Let Go".

The Sex Chakra is next. It is located on the pubic area. It controls and energizes the sexual organs and the bladder. Malfunctioning of this chakra manifests as sex-related problems. So we don't want this. Now that you aren't drinking anymore, and doing steps 1 through 9, you will probably notice a lot more virility in your sex chakra. If you are sexually active, then your partner will thank you. Continue the salt circle and "Let Go".

The Basic Chakra is located at the base of the spine or the coccyx area. The Basic Chakra controls, energizes and strengthens the whole physical body. The muscular and skeletal systems, the spine, the production and the quality of the blood produced, the adrenal glands, the tissues of the body and the internal organs. The Basic Chakra affects and energizes the sexual organs, body heat, general vitality and the growth of infants and children. People with highly activated basic chakras tend to be healthy while less active basic chakras tend to be fragile and weak. It's like the roots of a tree, which is why it is also known as the Root Chakra. If the roots are weak, then the tree is weak. So it's obviously a good idea to keep this chakra cleared. "Let Go".

Once you do salt circles on all your main chakras, then you can just scrub all over the rest of your body. Make sure you get the armpits and the other areas where the sun doesn't shine. Just cover your whole body and stand outside of the water flow and continue to chant "Let Go" for a couple of minutes. Then wash all the salt off with soap. You may also enjoy the coarseness of the salt to give you an extra scrub.

When you clean the dirty energy out of your chakras like this, it can be incredibly beneficial for your aura. If you maintain a healthy aura, then your physical body also maintains its health. Try it. You will thank yourself.

Step 11

Pick up a new hobby

I recommend learning how to play an instrument. Any instrument. Learn to play the guitar, the piano, the ukulele, the harmonica, or even the spoons. Something. Anything.

Even if you aren't musical, you can try. Start by giving yourself five minutes a day to practice. Anyone can find five minutes out of his or her day. And if you do this, you will be amazed at what you can accomplish in a very short time.

I had a few friends who played guitar when I was growing up, but I never learned how to play back then. I thought it seemed really hard and it hurt my fingers. Over the years I always had this feeling that it was too late to start, because I didn't learn when I was young. I just let time pass me by, and I would let everyone else play while I would sit back and sing. So I didn't even start playing until I was in my 30s. Once I finally picked it up and felt myself getting better and better, there was no turning back. Now I can play. I'm no virtuoso, but I can play. I rarely let a day go by that I don't play for a little while. I can still feel myself improving every time I play too.

Learning to play the guitar is one of the greatest things I have ever done for myself. I have to give my ex-girlfriend credit for encouraging me to learn. When we met, she had been playing for about a year and had already come pretty far. She used this same five minutes a day sales pitch on me. I thought if this woman can do that in a year, then I should be able to do the same or better. After all, I already knew music from singing all my life, so I just needed to take the time to do it. And since she had been able to work through the pain in the fingers, now my masculinity was at stake. So I finally picked it up, and I'm so thankful that I did.

Playing guitar has helped me tap into other sides of myself that I didn't even know existed before. I've written numerous songs and recorded some here and there. I've learned how to play well enough that I can jam with others. There is nothing cooler than that for me. It has given me such an incredible sense of accomplishment.

Now that I'm good enough to play my own songs, or I can learn other people's songs somewhat quickly, it's just such an awesome feeling. Even if I'm the only one who hears it, I still get the joy of being able to play for myself.

Also playing an instrument activates your brain in ways that will blow you away. Just watch the TedEd video on YouTube called "How playing an instrument benefits your brain". Playing an instrument is the brain's equivalent to a full body workout. How cool is that? That video says it all. It's less than five minutes, and it's animated too, so check it out.

If you already play an instrument, then you can stop playing drunk and actually get good now. We all know that alcohol has played a huge part in rock music. But if you play in front of people, then the audience doesn't want to watch you stumble around and fumble through songs. Even Keith Richards keeps his shit together during show time.

If you are not musical at all, and you think you can't learn any kind of instrument, then find something else creative that you can do. Paint, sing, draw, write, dance, sculpt, or build. Just find something that inspires you. Or learn how to find inspiration in something. We should all be dancing more actually. Even if you're by yourself, dance is very therapeutic. "Dance like no one is watching" because most likely they aren't watching. It will feed your soul, and you will have another reason to get up in the morning. Oh yeah, and you won't be hung-over anymore when that happens. What a concept!

Step 12

Evaluate your relationships
(Especially the one with yourself)

Once you stop drinking, you will have to look at all the people in your life and decide if they are helping you or hurting you. If you are anything like me, then you have probably collected a few drinking buddies along the way. These have become your "best friends" because they are always there when you need them, to drink with you. You have the common bond of booze.

And this is not to say that you can't develop strong friendships with these people. I'm still good friends with some of my old drinking buddies, but for the most part, I have moved on to higher vibration friendships. My relationships now have become much deeper, and are based on way more than just alcohol.

When you first stop drinking, this may be a very strange transition. It definitely was for me. I sort of became a hermit for the first few months. It almost felt like I didn't even know how to interact with people without having alcohol as part of the equation. I was also pretty embarrassed by the events that made me quit drinking, and I just didn't want to run into anyone that I knew. This alone time was actually pretty crucial to my healing process, and I recommend it for you too. You still need to be around people though, so don't completely isolate yourself.

Self-reflection is a powerful tool, and it was great for me to deal with my issues. This was the time when I started to pay attention to me. Not the other me that I used to know, but the new me that had to figure out how the hell to function in an alcohol infested society. I was so accustomed to being in bars and at parties, and now these weren't going to be my hangs anymore.

I was being forced to reassess my situation and all of my relationships. If someone reached out to me to find out where I had been hiding, I had to decide if this was a true friend that was looking out for my best interests, or if they were just looking for their old drinking buddy. For the most part, those that reached out were coming from a good place, and understood that I needed to make this change for myself. I also think that my desire to quit drinking was somewhat inspirational to some of my friends, and ultimately led to some of them quitting as well.

Finding your tribe of like-minded people can be very beneficial for the recovery process. AA is great for this aspect since you can find your tribe anywhere in the world where there is a meeting. It's like knowing that you can find a family wherever you go. That must be a pretty cool thing to know if you feel like you are not in control of your addiction and need others to keep you on track. If you are in the AA program or are considering it, then I would say that those relationships are probably pretty safe.

But the purpose of this book is for you to feel in control of your addiction because you're on the healthy path. And once you make that choice, then it is like a snowball effect. I will say it again, that one healthy choice leads to another. In the same way that one drink leads to another.

So now it's important to surround yourself with you. To do only what is best for you. If these old relationships suffer through this process, then that's probably a good thing. You don't need toxic people in your life. I realize this can be very difficult for many people, but it's the best thing for you and your recovery. I have still had to cut certain relationships out of my life almost eight years after I stopped drinking. It's not easy, but it has ultimately been for the best. Toxic people can be just as bad for you as alcohol. So get rid of the toxic energy. Surround yourself with happy people and it will rub off on you too.

The new people that I have attracted into my circle are incredible. It's so fun to feel proud of the friends that you have. I remember feeling embarrassed by certain people in my old circles. I knew that I couldn't introduce certain people to each other, because they just wouldn't get along. I don't feel that way anymore with my strongest relationships. This is most likely because they are on the same wavelength as I am. Trust this process, and trust your new mind set to attract the best people into your life. Find your new tribe of non-drinkers and notice how much less drama you will have as a result.

Step 13

Remove all the toxins in your life
(Cigarettes first)

Now, I'm going to assume that if you were a big drinker, then you most likely picked up smoking along the way too. And if you didn't pick it up, then you are lucky that you don't have to figure out how to quit. If you are a smoker, then I'm sure you are probably still holding on to this habit. That's why I saved this one for a later step.

Cigarettes are obviously not easy to quit. We all know this. But if you aren't a smoker then you don't understand how hard it is to quit. Let me tell you; it's a son of a bitch!

I used to love smoking cigarettes. I would relish

that alone time in the mornings. I loved the camaraderie that came with hanging in a group either outside of a bar or at work. Just smoking our lungs out. Those times were great. Going out for that smoke break at work was relaxing. After a meal or after sex were my favorite times to smoke. I loved all of it.

And I was a somewhat conservative smoker. I would say on average I was a half a pack a day smoker. Although when I was drinking it was more like a full pack. So to be honest, since I was drinking all the time, it was more like a full pack a day. So it wasn't too bad compared to a lot of people. I was also a conscious smoker. If there were people around who weren't smokers, I would try to be considerate and move away from them. Because I knew even then that the habit is disgusting. I was aware that it wasn't fair to subject others to my foul habit.

Quitting smoking doesn't have to be as hard as everyone makes it out to be. They say it's harder to quit than heroin. I've never done heroin, but if that's the case, then I'm sure I could quit heroin because I quit cigarettes. And I quit them for good.

What I came to terms with ultimately is that I had an oral fixation and I also liked the idea of taking these little mental breaks and going outside to breathe. But really it was more about going to feed my body poison. Just inhaling this poison for someone else's financial gain. It seems so silly to me now, but that's because the addiction doesn't have control of me anymore.

When you logically think about this little habit ruling your life and costing you all this money, it just doesn't make a damn bit of sense. Especially when you don't even make that much money, and you are spending your hard-earned dollars on actually taking years off your life.

Why would anyone in his right mind do this? Well probably because you weren't in your right mind yet. Because all these poisons are controlling you. It makes me sad to see people who are obviously poor, putting money into the pockets of corporate giants, who are making a fortune off of those people's addictions.

As we all know, nicotine is the primary psychoactive chemical in cigarettes, and it is highly addictive. Nearly half of cigarette smokers die of tobacco-related disease and lose 14 years off of their life on average. Not to mention all of the other toxins and chemicals that are in cigarettes. So again, why would we do this? Because when we are addicts, our bodies are not in control of our brains.

So here's how I quit. It started with the desire to quit. Then it was a gradual process of weaning off the nicotine. I did this with an electronic cigarette. For me, this worked like a charm. It felt just like smoking to me, and I was still getting the nicotine. But what I wasn't getting anymore was the smoke.

This is where the habit changed for me. Once I didn't smell like smoke anymore, I started to realize how horrible regular smokers smelled. And I also had the ability to vape my e-cig pretty much anywhere I wanted. So now I didn't have to go take those little mental smoke breaks anymore. I could just hit the e-cig whenever I felt like it.

It was also a lot cheaper to buy the e-juice. And I felt better about not giving my money to big tobacco companies anymore. I actually started to feel healthier too since I wasn't inhaling smoke and all the other chemicals from cigarettes.

This lasted for about two years. And that little e-cig had become like a little pacifier. But hey, I wasn't a smoker anymore. Now I was a vaporizer. And this felt healthier for a while even though I was still very addicted to nicotine. In my head though, I still hadn't lit and inhaled a cigarette since that desire to quit.

These days you will see a lot of people who have taken the vape thing to a whole new level. They have the huge batteries and blow huge clouds. Fortunately for me, I never took it to this next level. There is information out there about the dangers of vaping particular liquids, and it isn't good. "Popcorn lung" is the term used for what can happen to your lungs if you vape the bad e-juice. Most of that e-juice is toxic just so you know.

As fate would have it, I lost my e-cig. And that was it for me. At that point, the habit was so different. I didn't go outside and fraternize with the other smokers anymore. I didn't have to go somewhere to take that little break anymore either. Smoking altogether just lost its appeal. I was just buying this liquid nicotine and inhaling it because I was still addicted to the oral fixation and nicotine. So once I lost that e-cig, I decided right then that I didn't need to be addicted to nicotine anymore. So I quit for good that day, and I haven't had the urge for nicotine since. I did still enjoy vaping cannabis from time to time and that was a healthier choice for me.

The healthy choice to stop smoking and switch to vaping, led to the next choice to just stop nicotine altogether. And I don't miss it for a second. Now when I'm around cigarette smoke, I get pretty agitated. However, weed smoke is a different story. That doesn't seem to bother me.

Another way to help you quit smoking today is to vape your vitamins. I will vape B12 vitamins now. This seems to be a pretty new thing to vape vitamins, but I'm all for it. This is an excellent alternative to quitting cigarettes, and you can get a little boost of energy at the same time. There is a company called 'breathe' and their website is (www.breatheb12.com).

I know Alcoholics Anonymous does not support the use of cannabis with THC, but I don't know how they feel about using straight CBD for pain and inflammation. CBD alone does not get you high, and even my own mother is currently using it to help with neuropathy pain relief. There are so many benefits to this plant, and it can help with addictions too. There are still a lot of misconceptions around this subject. I know AA does not see this the same way when it comes to cannabis, which is another reason why that program did not appeal to me personally.

I will admit that I'm okay with cannabis use as a medicine. It's not for everyone, but it works for many others and me personally. Cannabis activates the biological endocannabinoid system, which serves a vital purpose for our health and wellbeing. It regulates key aspects to our biology. We are all seeing the tides turn on this plant as more and more states are finally legalizing it. I won't get into all the benefits of cannabis here, but if you don't know, then start doing some research. It's medicine, and there is a reason it has been on this planet for thousands of years. It's probably been here for millions of years actually. But I digress.

Start getting rid of the aluminum filled deodorants, the toxic cleaning supplies, the laundry detergents, the fluoride toothpaste, the harmful dyes and so on. There are healthy options for everything, and if you care to make these changes, you will figure them out. I recommend health food stores for most of these alternatives. Online is always an option too of course. There is a great online organic delivery company called

Thrive Market (www.thrivemarket.com) that is worth looking into. They only sell organic products that are priced below market value, and they deliver right to your door. They also help those in need as well.

You've probably never thought or cared about these things before, but now that you have made all the other major changes, you will start to notice all these other things around that are slowly killing us too. If you avoid these toxins, this is just one more way you can help to elongate your life.

Step 14

Enjoy live music

This step could be tough for people that may feel temptation around certain environments. However, now that you are incorporating these changes into your life, you shouldn't feel tempted to drink booze. Because if you are drinking that water, and meditating, and eating better, and exercising, and avoiding those toxic people, and writing, and hanging in nature, you will be able to be in these tempting environments with no problems.

When I first stopped drinking, I tried to avoid bars like the plague. I thought I would feel too much pressure to drink. After all, the bartenders would have my 'Joshtail' poured before I even sat down sometimes. But over time I actually didn't mind being in bars again. It's not my preference, but I can handle it now. It's usually harder for the people that are drinking to handle my not drinking. Back in the day, I wouldn't have trusted that guy not drinking either. But today I don't really care what others think. It just doesn't matter because whatever thoughts they may have about me is on them.

So these days I have grown to prefer music venues. Which is weird now looking back, because I have always enjoyed live music. Ever since I was a little kid. I didn't think twice about skipping Halloween when I was 8 years old to go see Barry Manilow (don't judge me) in concert. So I'm not sure what happened along the way, but I stopped going to see music and started hanging out in bars instead.

Once I stopped drinking, I realized how much more fun it was to go see live music or theater. I often enjoyed going to shows by myself. I still do. It's so fun to be a stranger in the crowd and to not know anyone. Even when I'm alone, I still feel a connection to the other people there. It's important to connect to your fellow man even if you aren't necessarily talking to them. It's still a form of fellowship or church.

You will probably start to notice how silly those people that are totally wasted really look. Now that you are not drinking, your judgment is clearer. You will also start to wonder how it is that you used to drink the way you did. And you will realize how much time you wasted doing this to yourself. You see that guy or girl that is falling down drunk? That used to be you. Be thankful that you are not that person anymore.

Every time I see someone wasted like that now, I just tap my chest and thank my higher power for allowing me to see the light. This enforces the positivity of this decision that I made for myself, and therefore does not make me want to drink. When you get to this point, you are home free in my opinion.

Everyone has a completely different relationship with addiction so you may have a tougher time. I think when you see others that haven't seen the light yet it brings clarity. And clarity brings power. Power to be free from your past and to be in the current moment. This is where true enlightenment comes from. Feel this moment. Take a deep breath and let it out. Nice right?

Music to me is the highest form of creative expression. I have dabbled in most creative outlets from acting to singing to writing or to dancing, and music is like a mainline directly to the heart. This is why I recommend going to see live music. I also recommend opening your mind to the possibilities of going to see music that you normally wouldn't necessarily go to.

For example if you are only into classical music I would suggest going to see some electronic dance music. And vice versa. The crowds will obviously be quite different. However, trust me when I say that you will be impressed by the kinds of sounds that are being made these days. And in the electronic scene, you will see the craziest visuals you can imagine. I was never into electronic music until I went to a festival that woke me up to this whole new world that I just didn't understand before. It's pretty powerful stuff. The bass can be so huge that it will vibrate you to your core. It will almost force you to dance.

Festivals are awesome because you are forced to

be outside enjoying nature, but you also come in contact with so many different types of people as well. Going to a festival alone can be an incredible experience too. I've done it a few times and always have a blast. Especially the types of festivals that have a variety of music mixed with art, yoga, and workshops. These are the best festivals because there is usually a raised consciousness that allows for an overall experience. Although they can all be pretty great if you are into the music.

Or maybe you are only into hard rock. How about trying on some bluegrass for size? These guys will blow you away with their musical skills, and you may just find that you enjoy this genre too, even though you may not have thought you would.

No matter what music you are into, if you ever get the chance to see Punch Brothers, Phish, Radiohead, Martin Sexton, I'm With Her, Dead&Co, String Cheese Incident, or Marcus Eaton you should just go. Even if you think it's not your style. These are some of the best musicians you will ever see. And you will also see what enjoying music really looks like. Trust me. I was never into Phish until I saw them live. These guys are truly at the top of their game. Of course, there are tons of other bands or artists that I could suggest, but it's a matter of taste and what you're into. The main thing is that you get out and go support live music because it's good for your heart and good for your soul.

However, if you think you will be too tempted to party then maybe you should avoid this until it doesn't faze you to be in these settings. If you're not ready yet, then just listen to more music in general. Music heals. And if you are one of those people who don't really get into music, then find something else that feeds your soul.

Step 15

Give back

Volunteer your time to help those in need. Give money if you have it. Get involved with a group or community of givers. This feeds your soul while you help others. This will take some effort since you will still be trying to come to terms with the new version of yourself.

AA is great for helping others within the AA community. I think it's a huge part of how AA does work. However, I feel like it mostly helps people with their sobriety. Obviously, that is extremely important, but if you get to this sobriety step sooner by improving your health habits, you will be able to help people that have issues that aren't related to just sobriety.

My friends in AA always seemed so busy with

activities that I couldn't imagine how they were able to focus on others. Or how they had time to talk to a sponsor or be a sponsor for someone else. That just seemed like too much work to me.

Not that there is anything wrong with work, I just didn't want to get tied down with all these attachments. Maybe this is good for addicts to have some accountability, but I just feel like it's a lot of plates to spin.

So give back to those that really need it and not only the people who are trying to stay sober. You will really start to feel your heart opening up when you do this. You will also generate good karma for yourself and your family by doing this. That's one of the many benefits that will come from giving back.

As a heavy drinker, I'm sure you didn't make much time for volunteering. You were probably too busy drinking. Well, now you have more free time to do something good for the world. Or maybe you feel inspired to write a book. Or do some public speaking. Or become a health coach. Or feed the homeless. Or become a big brother or big sister. Who knows? The sky is the limit when you allow yourself to be free from the clutches of your addictions.

Step 16

Breathe

Okay, I know we already covered meditation, but breathing, in general, is something that we all need to pay more attention to. Obviously, we don't need to think about breathing, but when you do, it has incredible benefits.

If you have never heard of Wim Hof and his breathing techniques, then you should look him up. He has brought some amazing things to light about the power of the breath and the capacity to become practically superhuman. Wim has developed the ability to withstand extreme conditions simply by taking in huge amounts of oxygen to the brain. And by extreme, I'm talking about staying under ice water for two hours, or hiking Mt. Everest in his shorts.

This dude is awesome, and he is totally inspiring.

He claims that we can all train ourselves to do this in a very brief time. There are some great YouTube™ videos that show people going through the process and seeing some crazy results.

It's also exciting to see just how easy it is too. He basically has you take 25-30 huge breaths in and out before holding your breath for as long as you can. Be careful though. You will probably feel some tingling and possibly emotions that you don't expect. You will be shocked at how long you can hold your breath for after trying this.

Apparently doing this alkalines the body and can be tested with strips in the mouth too. I have started incorporating these huge breaths into my daily routines, and it feels pretty great so far. I'm not ready for the ice baths or the frozen shirtless hikes yet, but I like the idea of becoming superhuman. I'm going to stick with it and see what happens.

If you're not ready to become superhuman, then you can start small. By just checking in with your breath whenever you think about it, is actually very beneficial too. I try to do this whenever I'm feeling grateful. Which is quite often these days. Anytime I have the feeling of gratitude; I will stop, take a deep breath in through my nose filling up my belly, and just tap my heart while I breathe out. Once I recognize this feeling, I will take a few deep breaths and then move on.

Another easy breath pattern I learned from Dr. Andrew Weil is to breathe in through your nose for a count of four, then hold this in for a count of seven, then breathe out for a count of eight. Try it and see how it feels. I dare you.

I have started doing this pattern right before I go to sleep at night and it has been great for helping me get to sleep. My sleep has been quite deep since I started this.

Step 17

Be grateful

Have gratitude. "Always look on the bright side of life" as they say in Monty Python. We can all be grateful for something. No matter how bad your life may seem you are alive on planet earth. It's a gift to be alive in this day and age.

With all the awesome technology and information that we have available, it's pretty easy to be grateful if you just stop and think about it. However, you have to stop and think about it.

Most of us are too busy focusing on the things we don't have or the things that just plain suck about life. So gratitude is a skill that needs to be practiced. According to Wikipedia, the systemic study of gratitude within psychology only began around the year 2000. This is probably because psychology traditionally focused more on understanding distress than on understanding positive emotions.

Well, now we know that expanding the science and practice of gratitude has consistently improved symptoms of illness, including depression, more optimism and happiness, stronger relationships, more generous behavior, and many other benefits. Water can be blessed with gratitude and will make the most beautiful patterns on the molecular level. Check out Dr. Masaru Emoto's work on this idea. It is fascinating. Since we are up to 70% water, if you apply these grateful thought patterns to your water, it will affect you on a molecular level. (Apply to step 1)

Many people say grace before meals, and that is a great thing to do. Even if you aren't religious, you can appreciate your food and where it comes from. That is also great for your digestive system to prepare for the food that you are about to receive.

Another great thing to do is to keep a gratitude journal. Doing this helps you to recognize all the positive things in your life, and also helps you develop this skill.

Think about three things that you are grateful for right now. It's not too hard to do. Right? Now keep it up. Tap your heart while you think of these things. It's a good reminder of the importance of your beating heart. And a beating heart is something to be grateful for! Hey how about that, now you only need to think of two more things.

Only good can come from having gratitude. There are apps now to help you with this too if you need some reminders. In fact, I'm downloading one right now called Grateful. I need to practice this more for myself, and now I have an app to help. You gotta love technology. The future is now. So be grateful.

Step 18

Get comfortable
with your sexuality

Sexuality is a subject that can be discussed at great length and should be. However, I am not an expert on this subject. Someone who is an expert that is worth looking into is Amy Jo Goddard. She really makes sense of the idea of sexuality. Sexuality encompasses so many different facets of who we are. It's not just about sex. It's about your creative self too. It's about expressing your true self. As Amy points out, when you think about it, we come into this world with zero knowledge of sexuality and have to figure it out on our own. That's a pretty crazy thing to think about since it can be so complex for so many people.

I will just say for myself that I have had some amazing relationships, and some not so amazing relationships in my life so far. I am a work in progress like all of us. In the past, I have made some really stupid decisions when it comes to sexuality. Can you guess what state of mind I was in when I made those stupid decisions? You guessed it. Wasted.

I'm sure that you have had your share of drunken stupidity when it comes to sexuality too. And if you were drinking like a fish, then I'm sure you have some stories you may regret too. I certainly do, but that's another book.

Everything that's happening with the 'Me Too' movement has really started to shine a light on the fact that so many people are still so confused when it comes to sexuality. Men especially have a lot to learn with this subject. It's still so shocking to hear about all of this moronic behavior. And the numbers keep growing. These are smart, educated, successful men that still have no idea how to read simple cues from a woman. Why is this? Well, where did they get their education on how to treat women and children? That's where the problem starts. If they are taught abuse at a young age, then they will probably pass on this behavior later in life.

Obviously, drugs and alcohol have a huge part to play in all of this ridiculous behavior too. I am in no way supporting any of the men that have been ousted recently, but I can't help but think about how much of an asshole I was when I was drinking. I'm certain that I never hurt anyone intentionally. But then again, I don't remember many nights.

Some of the nights I don't remember at all, I was later told what I had done, and I was mortified. I would have never done these things sober. So if these guys were wasted, then it's hard to say how much control they even had over their own behavior. This doesn't make it right at all, but I can definitely say that there were nights when I was drunk that I might have made an unwarranted pass or two. This obviously happened because I was too drunk to notice or care about any cues I was receiving. So many times, this happens for men, and it stems from the fact that they are not coming from a sober, conscious state.

Now that I have removed the alcohol, and have become so much more comfortable without it, it allows me to resonate on a different level. Now I am attracting the right type of energy my way. Since I am not seeking out women who drink, I don't have to deal with the confusion of not knowing what the woman wants. It's amazing how open the conversation can be when both parties are sober. It doesn't clarify all of our differences obviously, but it certainly is a better place to start a dialogue from.

By coming to terms with this new you, it allows you the ability to understand your own sexuality. This may take some time for you. Working on yourself doesn't happen overnight. It's a process. But if you take the time to do this work on yourself, the long-term effects will be evident. The next person that you attract into your life will be so much better for your own sexual understanding too. You will have better sex too. I can't guarantee this, but if you are both coming from a sober place, then it will definitely be better than drunken sex.

I would also highly suggest trying to remove porn from your habits. You don't watch porn you say? Sure, ya don't. If you are a man, then we all know you watch it. If you are a woman then you probably just don't want to admit that you watch it. I'm sure there are exceptions to the rule, but the bottom line is that too many people turn to porn for their sexual education. Which is like watching T-ball to learn how to be a professional baseball player.

They aren't even close to being in the same league.

I understand the visual nature of men specifically, but it is not healthy to assume that women want to be treated the way that most porn shows us they do. The other thing that most people don't realize about porn is that when you watch it, you attach energetic chords to these porn actors. This is not good for your aura. Because even though you can't see the chords, it shows up in your energetic field as people that you have been intimate with. Just take a break for a while and use your own fantasies if you need to 'rub one out'. You will feel better about yourself if you do this.

Getting in touch with your sexuality is about being empowered and confident in who you are and what you want. It's about treating yourself and others with respect. Once you start to understand this part of yourself, then you will also start to look and feel much sexier. Which will attract an equally sexy counterpart.

Step 19

Maintain a healthy mouth

This step should probably be much earlier because 80% of health problems start in the mouth. Oral health is something that we all take for granted, as we don't think about our mouth until there is a problem. Well, our oral microbiome is entirely connected to the overall health of our bodies. It is SO important to take care of our mouths. After all, think about how close it is to the brain.

I mentioned oil pulling with coconut oil earlier and it should be examined again here. There are absolutely incredible benefits to oil pulling and it can be done every morning when you wake up. It is antimicrobial and helps to remove bacteria from the mouth. It helps with infection, it whitens teeth, and it even tightens your gums. It's really amazing all the good that comes from oil pulling. All you have to do is swish it around in your mouth for fifteen to twenty minutes and then spit it out. Just don't spit it in your sinks or toilets. Adding essential oils like clove, lemon or oregano are also great too. You only need to add a few drops. You will see dramatic results to your health by making this a daily habit. You will also feel the difference in your mouth.

"The Mouth Body Connection" is a book by Gerald Curatola DDS. He is a holistic dentist that makes sense of the oral microbiome and the importance of proper oral hygiene. He also uncovers the lid on the dangers of fluoride, which I had been hearing about for years. It's great to finally hear it directly from a dentist. He has developed natural non-fluoride toothpaste that I use, and it is great. It's called Revitin, and it has vitamins and prebiotics that help your mouth instead of hurting it. Check out Gerry Curatola to find out more. He is the expert and sheds much-needed light on the mouth body connection. He actually claims that you don't need to oil pull if you use his Revitin toothpaste. But I still like the way it makes my mouth feel.

Fluoride is not good for us. We have been fed this lie that it is good for us for far too long. Fluoride is an industrial waste byproduct. It is not a pharmaceutical grade additive like we have been told. It's a poison that has been in our water supply since 1945.

As aluminum production increased in the first half of the twentieth century, it became necessary to find somewhere to put the fluoride. Manufacturers could no longer dump it into rivers or landfills, because it was poisoning crops and making livestock sick. So it wound up being added to our water and sold to us as something that is good for our teeth. It does zero good for our teeth. In fact, it harms them and the rest of our bones. Convincing the general public that we needed to add fluoride to our water supply was one of the most sophisticated cons of all time.

So it's time to get rid of the fluoride toothpaste for starters. Apparently there is enough fluoride in standard toothpastes to kill small children if it is swallowed. How crazy is that? Why would we want to put that in our mouths? Fluoride is also found in bottled water, which is another reason to avoid bottled water (See step 1). Do your own research on fluoride if you have doubts.

The main thing to be concerned about for mouth health, is what you are eating and drinking. If you have cut out all the processed sugar and junk food, then you are on the right path already.

Tooth decay is caused by three main factors. 1. Improper oral hygiene 2. Junk foods and high-carbohydrate foods 3. High acidic drinks like soda. (Good thing you gave up those Jack & Cokes, right)?

So it's time to pay closer attention to your oral health and get away from that fluoride. Start oil pulling if it suits you and don't forget to floss. This will be great for your overall health and wellbeing.

Step 20

Get out of your
own way

    This is a call to action and the final step. It is meant to encourage you to stop thinking about yourself all the time. You see self-love and self-care are what steps 1 through 19 are all about. You are the most important love in your life. If you are in love with yourself, then you can allow the right kind of love into your life. We have all heard this, but it is totally true. You can't properly love someone else until you learn how to love yourself. That is the main point of this book.

    However, now that you have figured out self-love, it's time to take it off yourself and start really noticing everyone else. Not just your loved ones but every single person on this planet. We are all one. We are all connected. There is only one race (that we know of) on this planet and that is the human race. So get used to that because it's not changing anytime soon. If you have racist tendencies, then change that shit right now. It does no good for the human race or the planet. We are all different, but we are still the same.

So now it's time to get out of your own head and start caring about everyone else too. This will take time, but it will make you a much happier person ultimately. Neal Donald Walsh spoke at a festival I went to years ago, and he said something that stuck with me. He said, "Any time that you enter a room you should silently say, I am here to heal the room. There is no other reason for me to be here." Talk about taking it off of yourself! Another awesome quote of his is "Your life has nothing to do with you. It is about everyone whose life you touch and how you touch it". If we all think in that way, we can start to change the world. And now that you have changed yourself, you can start to heal the world too. Whatever that means to you.

For me, this has translated into a desire to go to the Institute for Integrative Nutrition™ to become a health coach. Which led to me writing this book. As a creative person, I have always found joy in the process of creating. However, it was always all about me when I was trying to find success. After awhile. I started to feel like I wasn't making any sort of difference in people's lives. That's why I want to help others like you come to terms with your own issues.

When I was drinking, I was never in a position where I could really think about helping others. Meditation has been the main reason that I think my soul has started to evolve and has taken the focus off of me. Hopefully, this will happen for you too. Not that you will have to change your life around completely, but maybe it will help you shift the focus off of yourself to some degree. Compassion can become a passion if you allow it to. So get out of your own way and allow the flow of good karmic energy to resonate within you.

In case you lost count that was 20 steps. I realize it's eight more steps than a 12-Step program. However, these steps should not take you nearly as long to accomplish. The beauty of my system is that you are the only one holding yourself accountable for this. It isn't about having to show up for anybody else but you.

So, how do you start? Well that's the million-dollar question that only you can answer. Do you need to hit your 'rock bottom' first or can you make the changes before that happens? Most addicts need that wake up call. I hope this book helps to encourage you to wake up before the call comes in. Before too much damage is done. If it's too late and the damage is already done, then you have your excuse to change today. But hopefully you have already started making changes.

If you are still on the fence about making these changes, then just get off the fence and do it. Right now. Start with one step at a time. If you look at the table of contents of this book, then you could probably apply half of these steps tomorrow. It's not likely that you will see great results this way, but the steps are technically easy enough to start immediately. But you have to make that choice. I know change is hard, but staying in the position that you've been in will ultimately be much harder.

Maybe one of the reasons AA has become the most notable recovery program is because it does bring people together to work through these issues. There are benefits to this for many. I know there are many friendships that are also made this way, which is great. Especially when it comes to those who feel like they need this structure and these relationships.

For me, I feel empowered by the fact that I figured it out on my own. It didn't require as much work as I was expecting either. I just knew I had to stop drinking because I was hurting the people around me. Basically, once I came to that conclusion, it was just about sticking to my decision. I had to let my brain win the battle with my body.

It wasn't easy to give up all the fun at first. It was so hard to imagine how I was going to have any fun without booze. Although now I realize that it actually was a pretty easy thing to do once I learned to love myself. It was so obvious that I wasn't going to accomplish anything substantial in my life as long as I was drinking.

A whole new world of possibilities has opened up since I stopped being so selfish. I am considerably happier. I'm more open and generous. I never really stress about too much. I feel and look better than ever. I feel a tremendous amount of love for myself, and therefore I feel more love for others. Once you get yourself well, then you can help spread the love too.

It excites me to share this book with anyone who may benefit from it. I truly hope that it inspires you to join me on this journey of an alcohol-free life. If you join me, then I'm sure you will agree. And if you don't want to join me, then you keep doing you, if that's what makes you happy. But if you want to be a better you then make the changes.

And if you apply all these steps and you don't

see dramatic results, then you may need to seek out professional help or rehab. PLEASE do that if you need to! As I mentioned before, I'm not an expert. I'm just a guy who changed and I felt like I had to share how I did it. You deserve to be better and everyone else in your life deserves a better version of you too. You can do this! Godspeed and God Bless!

Feel free to reach out to me if you are interested in coaching. I would also like to hear how your life has changed if you apply these steps. I am also available for speaking engagements. My website is
(www.howtobeabetteryou.today)